REST

Stonecroft
where she is ✢ as she is

Rest is one of Stonecroft's *Conversations* series.

Unless otherwise indicated, all Scripture quotations are taken from the Holy Bible, New Living Translation, copyright © 1996, 2004, 2007 by Tyndale House Foundation. Used by permission of Tyndale House Publishers, Inc., Carol Stream, Illinois 60188. All rights reserved.

Designed and Typeset by Serena Lilli Jeanne

ISBN: 978-0-9908500-5-2

Produced and Distributed by:

Stonecroft
10561 Barkley Suite 500
Overland Park, KS 66212

800.525.8627 / connections@stonecroft.org

www.stonecroft.org

0316

Contents

Acknowledgments

New to the Conversation?   1

Tips for Guiding the Conversation   2

Conversation 1: Fast and Furious   3

Conversation 2: Struggling to Survive   9

Conversation 3: Take Me Away   15

Conversation 4: Far from Perfect   21

Rest Received   27

Intro to the Bible   33

Resources   36

Acknowledgments

Stonecroft is grateful for author Lorraine Potter Kalal, Stonecroft President and CEO, for her dedication and endless desire to know God better.

We also thank the team who provided prayer, editing, design, and creative input to see the Stonecroft *Conversations* series launched.

New to the Conversation?

Welcome to Stonecroft *Conversations* — a series of resources designed to inspire conversation around meaningful topics and introduce women to the Bible and Jesus Christ. This conversation focuses on something that many women long for: *Rest*.

If you are picking up a *Conversations* resource for the first time, welcome! We have some helpful tips for you. Someone, perhaps you, will need to guide the discussion. Don't worry; it's easy and we provide "Tips for Guiding the Conversation" on the next page. Don't know much about the Bible? Go to page 33 for some helpful background information on that historic spiritual book. We trust that as you and friends gather to discuss *Rest*, you'll have some thought-provoking, and perhaps life-affecting, dialogue.

We want to hear about it!

Questions?
Contact us at connections@stonecroft.org
or 800.525.8627.

We pray that this conversation makes a difference in your life and the lives of the women who join it!

– Stonecroft

Tips for Guiding the Conversation

Flexibility is key. Use *Rest* in a way that fits the needs of your group. Take as long as you need and skip questions if you want. Do the assignments or not! Make this work for you.

A few more thoughts:

- Pray. As a facilitator, take time to pray for your group and each participant before you get together.
- Ensure that each participant has her own copy of *Rest*. Visit stonecroft.org/store.
- Ask everyone to read together "Intro to the Bible" on page 33 or before your first meeting to gain background on the Bible.
- Facilitation doesn't mean you have to be an expert. Just ask someone to volunteer to read each paragraph aloud or simply read together silently. Then ask the questions and let conversation fly!
- Recognize that some may want to read and write their responses before you meet. Others may not. Same with the sections called "Reflect and Journal." These are questions that may help each woman go deeper between group meetings.
- Note that each week's conversation ends with prayer. You can read this aloud together or simply pray silently in your own words.
- You may wish to extend your meetings by a week to share what each of you has learned and to review the questions following the last section: "Rest Received." This is a helpful way to reflect on what you've experienced over the past few weeks.

For more information on guiding *Conversations*, visit stonecroft.org/conversations to download "Facilitating a Stonecroft Small Group."

Stonecroft offers a variety of resources, including additional *Conversations*. Go to stonecroft.org/store to learn more.

Conversation 1
Fast and Furious

Start the Conversation

1. What does the word "rest" mean to you? What feels like "unrest"?

2. Discuss the busy lives of women worldwide. What kind of pressures do women face? In what way might women need rest?

Her Story

Laura began her day scrambling to get her kids out the door to school, meet deadlines at work, rush home, make a semblance of a healthy dinner, pay bills, and then repeat the same thing every day. As a single mom, she felt overwhelmed and exhausted, wondering if her life would ever change. She sat down one night and while looking at Facebook, an online article about child laborers caught her eye.

She clicked and read about Lini who was 12 years old when she began working in a factory. It wasn't unusual for Lini to be there since her mother and aunts worked at the factory too. In fact, she and her siblings played games with the fabric scraps and empty spools of thread when they were little. Now that she was older, Lini worked to manufacture t-shirts for a European clothing company that increasingly put pressure on the workers to produce more. It upset her to see her mother crying when the boss abused her verbally, and sometimes physically, but Lini didn't know what to do and didn't want to lose her job. When she went to sleep in their small tin shack at night she felt overwhelmed and exhausted, wondering if her life would ever change. Her long work hours crushed Lini's desire to attend school.

Sitting there in her small but warm home, even in the midst of her tiredness and fears about her kids and life, Laura felt her throat tighten and tears well up in her eyes as she thought about Lini and her family. She knew things like this existed but felt hopeless to make any meaningful change in the world. She thought of her own kids and pushed the thought out of her mind that her oldest daughter was the same age as Lini. There were so many problems in the world and in her life, so much pain and sadness. Falling into bed that night, Laura thought about her childhood, when, after a day of playing outside with friends, she would go to bed happy and tired. Now she just felt alone and too overwhelmed to change her life, let alone the lives of children across the world. All Laura wanted right now... was rest. Rest from her own fast and furious life. And rest from worrying about everyone else's problems.

Do you relate?

1. How did you relate to either Lini's or Laura's story?

2. What can you do to rest? To help other women find rest?

Bible and Background

Don't forget to read "Intro to the Bible" on page 33 to get familiar with terms like "Exodus" and "Old Testament."

From Exodus 20:8-10
Remember to observe the Sabbath day by keeping it holy. You have six days each week for your ordinary work, but the seventh day is a Sabbath day of rest dedicated to the LORD your God. On that day no one in your household may do any work. ...

The Bible reveals that God set up a day called the Sabbath, a day when humans would rest after six days of work. Today Christians celebrate the Sabbath on Sunday. Jewish people observe it on Saturday. Muslims have a day of prayer on Fridays although they don't call it a Sabbath.

Religions agree: it's good to stop working! Give it a rest!

The Sabbath wasn't just one day of the week either. God told Israel to have a Sabbath every seven years — and to give the land a rest, too.

Leviticus 25:3-4, 6
For six years you may plant your fields and prune your vineyards and harvest your crops, but during the seventh year the land must have a Sabbath year of complete rest. It is the LORD's Sabbath. Do not plant your fields or prune your vineyards during that year. ... But you may eat whatever the land produces on its own during its Sabbath.

Later in this chapter of the Bible's book called Leviticus, God instructed Israel to take an even bigger rest every 50 years — during what's called the Year of Jubilee. The land rested from being planted for two years in the Year of Jubilee — but the poor were able to gather grain that grew on its own during those years.

The Year of Jubilee gave rest to the poor and also to those who owed money. If you were forced by need to sell land to someone, the owner returned the land to you during the Year of Jubilee. And if you were a bondservant — you worked for someone else without salary to pay off a debt — your master automatically released you during the Year of Jubilee. What was the effect of God's 50th year of rest on Israel?

> The Year of Jubilee prevented the Israelites from oppression of one another. … It had a leveling effect on Israel's culture by giving everyone a chance for a new start. It discouraged excessive, permanent accumulations of wealth and the depravation of an Israelite of his inheritance in the land. Families and tribes were preserved by the return of freed bondservants to their own families. Permanent slavery in Israel was rendered impossible.[1]

What did Jesus say about this rest that the Bible calls "Sabbath"? In Mark's biography of Jesus, the religious leaders accused Jesus' friends and followers of breaking the Sabbath, of not resting. They were "… breaking off heads of grain to eat" (Mark 2:23). Seriously? That violated the Sabbath? These leaders created all sorts of picky rules about how to rest. It was a lot of work to remember what you could or couldn't do on the Sabbath. People had to work in order to rest!

So how did Jesus respond to this accusation? He corrected the leaders by saying, "The Sabbath was made to meet the needs of people, and not people to meet the requirements of the Sabbath" (Mark 2:27).

God created the Sabbath to meet our needs, to give us time to stop, to cease, to rest — rest from work, rest from slavery, rest from debt, rest from poverty, and rest from worry. He even gave rest from trying so hard to follow all the rules — even the rules about how to rest!

> When we **rest**, we cease, we stop. God created the Sabbath to give people time to stop, to cease, to rest — rest from work, rest from slavery, rest from debt, rest from poverty, rest from worry.

I need rest.

---

[1] http://www.studylight.org/dictionaries/hbd/view.cgi?n=6487

How about you?

1. What surprised you about the Sabbath? Confused you? Encouraged you?

2. The Pharisees gave a lot of rules about how to rest. It took a lot of work to rest well! When do you "rest," but not really rest?

3. In what areas of your life would you like God to help you stop and rest? How do you think He could help you?

Talk to God

Read this prayer together or pray it silently — then add some of your own thoughts to God.

God,

It surprises me that you care about me getting rest. That you care about giving rest to the land, the poor, the debtors. I could use some rest. I'm not sure what you can do for me, but maybe you can help me to slow down, to set aside time to stop and take it easy. Maybe I can ask someone to give me a break, take the pressure off. Show me what to do. I need your help and I need rest. Thanks.

Amen.

Reflect and Journal

Think about rest during the week before the next conversation. Maybe it will help to write down some reflections below — or buy a journal to record your thoughts.

Write down areas in your life where you long to stop and rest.

_____
_____
_____
_____

List some activities that feel like rest to you.

_____
_____
_____
_____

How do you waste time "relaxing" in a way that simply numbs you, helps you avoid the pain?

_____
_____
_____
_____

Now, write down some ways you can take time to really rest instead.

_____
_____
_____
_____
_____

If you're comfortable, pray this week and ask God for insight about how you can find some rest. Perhaps you might read back over the Bible readings and write down any new observations or thoughts you have.

If you feel overwhelmed trying to find rest and want to know more about how Jesus gives you rest, check out "Rest Received" on page 27.

Conversation 2
Struggling to Survive

Start the Conversation

1. As you reflected about rest this week, what discoveries came to mind?

2. Share how you were able to stop and rest this past week. What helped you to rest? What didn't? What was difficult about resting or kept you from resting?

Her Story

I repeat the same mantra every single day: "Overwhelmed! Help!" There's just SO MUCH TO DO, so many things to worry about, so much weighs me down. And, so often, no one there to help in person.

I'm tired.

I have my job. I have my apartment. I have me. I have my cats. I have my car. Oh, and I have my kids.

I have to care for them all. That load increased after my husband left. So now I have the house, the bills, the taxes, the meals, the projects I never get around to that weigh on me. I stay up late fretting — or avoiding the pressure, the fear, the pain by surfing the internet or watching TV. Then it's up as early as I'm able to shuttle the kids to school and head off to work. The weekend for rest? You've got to be kidding! The chores pile up begging to be done.

Every day the questions overwhelm me: What did I forget to do? What do I need to do tonight? Is there food for meals? What work still looms in the apartment, with the bills, in our schedules? Every day I struggle against the demands.

What about all the decisions at work? The projects that threaten to bury me? The goals I must achieve, but fear I'll fail to finish? The people I won't please? The people I can't please?

The days, the pressure, the To Do lists engulf me. Depress me. I need rest.

I'm looking for someone, anyone, to take a load off, to care for me.

Will the struggle ever end? I need rest. Help!

Do you relate?

1. What struggles feel impossible for you to overcome, to stop and find rest? How does your situation affect your emotions and your body?

2. How do you quiet down your mind in order to rest?

Bible and Background

God made some pretty outrageous promises to people in the Old Testament. God told a man named Abraham that He would give him a huge family — though Abraham and his wife Sarah were too old to have children — that they would one day live in a beautiful, fruitful area called the Promised Land. Hundreds of years later, God repeated that promise to Abraham's descendants, the people of Israel (see Exodus 33:12-14).

God's promise included rest from Israel's enemies and rest in "a land flowing with milk and honey." Rest meant no more struggling for life — the struggle against enemies who wanted to destroy Israel and the struggle to find food. Rest meant peace and abundance, freedom from fear and famine. Rest meant an end to struggling and the start of satisfaction.

Hundreds more years passed before Israel found its rest. Israel entered the Promised Land. The people eventually took control of the territory, finding freedom from enemy nations, and enjoying the fruits of their labor.

The third King of Israel, Solomon, built a beautiful temple to honor God. As he prayed to dedicate the temple, Solomon remembered God's promise of rest. And he thanked God:

1 Kings 8:55-56
[Solomon] stood and in a loud voice blessed the entire congregation of Israel: "Praise the LORD who has given rest to his people Israel, just as he promised. ..."

A Psalm is a poetic song or hymn sung by the nation of Israel during worship. Many of the Psalms were written by Solomon's father, King David — who often sought rest from his enemies. Psalms 4 and 127 reveal a loving God who cares for His people, who deals with their struggles, giving them safety, abundant food, peace, sleep — rest.

Psalm 4:7-8

You have given me greater joy
than those who have abundant harvests of grain and new wine.
In peace I will lie down and sleep,
for you alone, O LORD, will keep me safe.

Psalm 127:2

It is useless for you to work so hard
from early morning until late at night,
anxiously working for food to eat;
for God gives rest to his loved ones.

How did Israel receive this rest? Sometimes they had to work — with God's help — to fight off their enemies and harvest their grain. Sometimes they prayed and God miraculously delivered food or victory. Sometimes God blessed His people just because they were His people.

The odd thing about Israel is that they didn't always want to receive God's rest. They didn't trust Him to give them rest. Or they didn't like how he relieved their struggles — like the time he gave them miraculous food called manna and they got sick and tired of it. God sadly reminded His people: "... 'Only in returning to me and resting in me will you be saved. In quietness and confidence is your strength. But you would have none of it'" (Isaiah 30:15).

> **Rest** meant no more struggling for life ... Rest meant peace and abundance, freedom from fear and famine. Rest meant an end to struggling and the start of satisfaction.

We desperately need rest. Rest from enemies. Rest from the struggle to meet our needs. Rest from struggling to survive. Sometimes we can't find it. Sometimes we refuse it.

How about you?

1. What is your Promised Land? How would your life be different if you found the kind of rest described in Psalms 4 and 127?

2. What would it take for you to feel at rest from your struggles, to feel secure and satisfied?

3. What would it feel like to trust God to take care of your struggles?

4. Israel sometimes rejected the rest God wanted to give them. When and why would you refuse or reject rest?

Talk to God

Here's a sample prayer you might use:

God,

Can you help me find rest from the things that weigh me down, from my daily struggles? There is so much to do, so much on my mind. I really like that you can help me to rest, that you can give me sleep. Can you help me to learn how to stop even when there's a huge To Do list? Thank you so much.

Amen.

Reflect and Journal

Perhaps you'd like to take some time this week to reflect on rest.

Write about challenges in your life that are so demanding you don't believe you can stop and rest.

_____
_____
_____
_____
_____

Write what it would feel like if someone came along and took care of your struggles.

_____
_____
_____
_____
_____

List some things you can put off until next week, then write down how you will rest instead.

_____
_____
_____
_____

Try to pray about these enemies of rest and ask God for help — like Israel did. Try this: Every night before you go to bed, write down all the things that you are worried about doing the next day — that overwhelming To Do list. Take that piece of paper and symbolically hand it to God. If you feel comfortable, pray that God takes these struggles off your mind and helps you sleep well.

If you feel overwhelmed right now and long for God to care for you like He did the people of Israel, check out "Rest Received" on page 27. Learn how you can have a closer relationship with the God who grants rest.

Conversation 3
Take Me Away

Start the Conversation

1. How did last week go? Share how you found rest...
   or not!

2. What's the ideal way you like to take time away from
   the rat race? Do you spend time alone or hang out
   with people?

Her Story

Sitting in the park on her lunch break, Tia gazed up at the trees. She had been inside all day working at her telemarketing job. People sat packed in a noisy room making phone calls to people who were rude and annoyed which filled her with stress and anger. She worked long hours in this tense place. When she got home, she was just too tired to have a social life. She was lonely and exhausted most of the time. She wished she had a friend to lean on, someone to share her burdens.

Tia had one break a day for lunch and took advantage of that time to get away and go outside to a nearby park. As she sat and rested, sunlight filtered through the green leaves and she sighed wishing she had a window to look out of at work. She grabbed her phone and took a picture of the trees. At least she could look at the photo on her phone even if there wasn't any sunlight in her office. Later after her boss yelled at her, she took out her phone and gazed at the picture, trying to summon the peace she felt when she looked at the trees.

This became a ritual for how Tia coped with the stress of her job — each lunch break she took a picture of something beautiful; sparrows splashing in a puddle, a vibrant red coat a woman wore, the strip of bright green grass, butterflies resting on one of the flowers in the planter on the sidewalk. These little glimpses of the pictures helped Tia remember that life was more than endless angry phone calls and colleagues who complained all day. She felt like the pictures were her friends, bringing her peace, calm, beauty, even rest. Even if she couldn't afford to take a real vacation, she could take her 20 minutes to find something beautiful to get her through the rest of the day.

Do you relate?

1. How did you feel as you read about the way Tia coped with stress?

2. How do you find rest even in pressure-filled situations?

Bible and Background

Psalm 23

The LORD is my shepherd;
I have all that I need.
He lets me rest in green meadows;
he leads me beside peaceful streams.
He renews my strength.
He guides me along right paths,
bringing honor to his name.
Even when I walk
through the darkest valley,
I will not be afraid,
for you are close beside me.
Your rod and your staff
protect and comfort me.
You prepare a feast for me
in the presence of my enemies.
You honor me by anointing my head with oil.
My cup overflows with blessings.
Surely your goodness and unfailing love will pursue me
all the days of my life,
and I will live in the house of the LORD
forever.

King David who wrote Psalms 4 and 127 from last week also wrote the beautiful Psalm 23. David was the same person who as a boy killed the nation's enemy Goliath with a slingshot. He certainly needed rest, especially from his enemies. King Saul — who ruled before David — constantly tried to kill David out of jealousy. And David's own son Absalom tried to overthrow him. In between, David led Israel in many battles against the nation's enemies. It seems like someone always attacked David.

Many of the Psalms are filled with David's complaints to God about his struggles, but they end with trust that his loving God would take care of David, would grant him peace... and rest. David even fell asleep in a cave once while surrounded by his enemies!

Psalm 23 beautifully shows David's trust in a God who walks with him like a shepherd cares for sheep — in tough times and good times. God walked close by David through valleys of death and difficulties. And God led David to rest on green meadows by mountain streams. God's love pursued David.

God gave Israel rest from her struggles — defeat of her enemies and provision of food. And God gave David a deeper rest — rest in his soul, knowing that God walked with him through everything. God guided, protected, comforted, and loved him.

Jesus Himself talked about that kind of rest in the Gospel of Matthew, another Bible book. He tells His followers — and He tells us — that He can give us rest, that He can share our burdens.

Matthew 11:28-30

> ... Jesus said, "Come to me, all of you who are weary and carry heavy burdens, and I will give you rest. Take my yoke upon you. Let me teach you, because I am humble and gentle at heart, and you will find rest for your souls. For my yoke is easy to bear, and the burden I give you is light."

Imagine two oxen yoked together. The yoke was a specially fitted piece of wood that lay on the shoulders of both animals. The oxen moved forward side-by-side to pull the weighty cart attached to the yoke. One of the oxen had more experience; he taught the younger "apprentice" ox how to pull the burden. Together, they made work lighter.

That's the picture Jesus draws of a relationship with Him. We aren't alone; He is tied to us night and day. He does the lion's share of the work as the more experienced ox. Together we face life's hurdles. He never leaves. When we rush ahead, He slows us down. (I imagine Him looking at me sideways as He stands still and I strain forward. He looks at me as if asking why I'm in such a hurry!) When we can barely move, He trudges forward, pulling us along. He knows when to go left and when to go right. All we need do is lean into His movements.

A **deeper rest** is a rest that derives from knowing that God walked with [David] through everything, that God guided, protected, comforted, and loved him.

How about you?

1. What about Psalm 23 and the quote from Matthew surprised you? What confused you?

2. How did you feel as you read Psalm 23? Think of a dear friend lovingly leading you by the hand through tough times and good. If you can recall such a time, how did that feel to you? If not, what would it mean to have a friend like that?

3. Imagine resting by a mountain pond, clear and calm. Where do you find that kind of rest in your daily life?

4. Picture yourself in a yoke with Jesus. He leads every step of the way. What does that thought stir in your soul?

Talk to God

Here's a sample prayer you might repeat aloud — or pray silently:

Dear God,

I am lonely. I am stressed. I am exhausted. I am hurt. I never stop feeling pressure. The Bible tells me that you can help, that you can be my shepherd who walks with me, that you restore my soul with your love. You can be the older ox who leads me and shares my burdens. The Bible tells me that you can give me rest. I'd like that. Would you mind helping me to receive and accept the rest you give? Thanks.

Amen

Reflect and Journal

Take a deeper dive into your need to rest this week. Read through Psalm 23 again. List your dark valleys, your enemies, your burdens, the things that dissatisfy.

_____
_____
_____
_____
_____

Maybe you long for a friend who will walk with you through life, who will help bear your load. Maybe you are angry because you have never had such a friend. Write it all down. Tell God. Perhaps you can ask Him to be that friend.

_____
_____
_____
_____
_____

David expressed his needs in the Psalms. And David found rest in God. If you don't have a Bible, you may want to download a Bible app so you can read some of the Psalms (try downloading an app that includes the New Living Translation which is easier to read). Read one of these Psalms each night before you go to bed to help you find rest like David did: Psalms 13, 32, 57, 51, and 121.

Write down your thoughts as you read.

_____
_____
_____
_____
_____

Does having God walk with you and take you to rest by cool streams sound good? Does having Jesus share the weight of life's burdens appeal to you? Check out "Rest Received" on page 27 to learn how you can have a friendship like that with Jesus.

Conversation 4
Far from Perfect

Start the Conversation

1. Talk about if and how you rested this past week. What helped you rest?

2. What are things you do before you go to bed at night? How do they help you to rest or not rest?

Her Story

Movies, magazines, Instagram, Facebook — wherever I look I see happy — possibly perfect — people. Sure, I can find the sad stories if I try, but my eye, my mind, my emotions focus on what I lack. I see smiling, complete people. I see gorgeous women. I see perfect homes. I see families with two parents, two put-together kids, a dog, a cat, and a fabulous vacation.

I see what I don't have.

The weirdest thing is this — a lot of the time I figure the reason I don't have the "American Dream" is because of me! I don't deserve any better. I'm just not good enough. I'm somehow broken. It's my fault that my life isn't perfect, or anywhere near that. I feel shame, hot searing shame.

On top of that, I live under a load of guilt. I never live up to my standards. I'm so easily irritated. Sometimes I snap. Even if others don't see it, I feel the anger inside. I forget to focus on other people. Or I let them walk all over me when somehow I know that's not right, either. Every single day, I let myself down. I know somehow I'm broken, but I don't know how to fix myself.

I'm worn out living under the pressure of shame, the burden of guilt.

I need rest.

Do you relate?

1. How do you feel after you've spent some time on social media?

2. What causes you to feel shame? What makes you guilty? What are ways you deal with the pressure?

3. Have your experiences with religion felt more like pressure and demands or more like rest? In what ways?

Bible and Background

Luke 11:46
Jesus [said to the "experts in religious law"], "... [You] crush people with unbearable religious demands, and you never lift a finger to ease the burden."

That sense that we're just not good enough. Those things we've done wrong. All that shame. All that guilt.

The religious leaders of Jesus' time had one solution — and it wasn't restful! They put together a long To Do list of religious demands. In effect they told the people, "Do these things and you'll be OK with God. All this work will make up for your guilt and shame." Do you feel their religious load bearing down, crushing you?

Jesus did. And He told them to stop. Jesus came to give us rest, not more work.

Hebrews 4:9
... there is a special rest still waiting for the people of God.

We talked in week 2 about God's promise that Israel could rest from struggling against enemies and to find food. Last week we discovered an experience of rest when a loving leader guides us to still waters or by sharing an easy, light yoke.

But the writer of the Bible book of Hebrews tells us that God promises an even deeper rest, a "special" rest — a rest from guilt, a rest from shame, a rest from striving to erase the shame and the guilt. Jesus came to bring that rest.

John 17:1-5
... Jesus looked up to heaven and said, "Father, the hour has come. Glorify your Son so he can give glory back to you. For you have given him authority over everyone. He gives eternal life to each one you have given him. And this is the way to have eternal life—to know you, the only true God, and Jesus Christ, the one you sent to earth. I brought glory to you here on earth by completing the work you gave me to do. Now, Father, bring me into the glory we shared before the world began."

Jesus did the work that grants us rest. Jesus prayed with His friends right before He was arrested and taken to be crucified. In this prayer, Jesus says that He has completed the work God wanted Him to do. That work was a perfect life that culminated in His death on a cross.

Why did Jesus have to die? The Bible says that Jesus died *for* us. We can see the ways that this world is evil and we know intuitively that we are broken, too, that we aren't perfect. The Bible calls our wrong thoughts and actions "sin."

The Pharisees had it right — sort of. We have to make up for sin. We sense we have to compensate by working hard to be good — or bear the consequences.

But here's the difference Jesus makes. He did the work for us. He endured our punishment and lived the perfect life for us. He worked so we can rest.

Jesus did this work so that we could have eternal life. Jesus defines "eternal life" as knowing God, having a deep, intimate, loving relationship with God that starts now and lasts forever. That's where we find rest.

Can you imagine someone who loves you so much He would let Himself be killed in your place? Can you imagine a love so deep, so free? That kind of love does something for a person. When you're loved that much, shame and guilt disappear. Guilt leaves when sins are forgiven — because someone else took the punishment for them. Shame leaves when you know you're loved deeply, a love that says, "I accept you, no matter what. And I will fix your brokenness."

Jesus can give anyone rest from sin, from shame, from guilt. He says there is only one thing required: to believe. Believe that Jesus is God and that He did all the work necessary for you to rest in His forgiving arms.

I needed rest from shame, from guilt.

> Jesus came to bring a **special rest**, a rest from guilt, a rest from shame, a rest from striving to erase the guilt and shame.

How about you?

1. As you reviewed the Bible quotes and background, what questions arose? What surprised you? What feelings did you have?

2. The Pharisees felt like they could work to make up for their sin. In what ways do you try to do the same thing?

3. The Bible says that the only thing God wants from us is to believe in Jesus. How is that different from what you previously thought about God?

Talk to God

Dear God,

I know that I'm not perfect. I feel inadequate a lot. I try to be a good person, to do my best. But I feel tired from all the ways I work at living a perfect life. And I feel bad when I fail. It all just wears me out. Can you help me receive some rest from you? Thanks.

Amen

Reflect and Journal

Write down times this week when you feel shame or guilt.

_____

_____

_____

_____

_____

_____

What do you do to compensate for your shame and guilt?

_____

_____

_____

_____

_____

_____

What do you think about Jesus' offer of rest?

_____

_____

_____

_____

_____

_____

Read "Rest Received" if you want to understand more about the special rest Jesus offers — and what you can do to receive it.

Rest Received

Start the Conversation

1. Take a moment to reflect on any obstacles that keep you from believing God can give you the kind of rest you long for.

2. What do you think God is trying to say to you through this conversation?

3. How have you encountered Jesus through the Bible and the stories?

What the Bible Says about Finding Rest

The Bible ends with huge hope. It tells us that sometime in the future everything reverses. This unjust, decaying, sad, selfish world of ours will be replaced by a new world that undoes all that's wrong and bad and fallen. God's people will experience complete rest. Read this hope-filled quote from the Bible:

Revelation 21:1-4

Then I saw a new heaven and a new earth, for the old heaven and the old earth had disappeared. And the sea was also gone. And I saw the holy city, the New Jerusalem, coming down from God out of heaven like a bride beautifully dressed for her husband.

I heard a loud shout from the throne, saying, "Look, God's home is now among his people! He will live with them, and they will be his people. God himself will be with them. He will wipe every tear from their eyes, and there will be no more death or sorrow or crying or pain. All these things are gone forever."

God gives His people the ultimate Sabbath — a place of rest where struggling and pain and sorrow cease and God walks with His beloved friends forever.

How do we enter the rest we long for? We receive rest now when we begin a deeply intimate and loving relationship with Jesus Christ that lasts forever.

What the Bible Says Jesus Did For You

Jesus loves people so deeply that He made a way for us to have that restful relationship with Him, the God of the Universe! It may seem backward, but instead of us having to work hard to live a good life to reach God, God did the work for us. He reached down to us through Jesus Christ to come get us and start that relationship — in spite of all we have ever done wrong, in spite of our sin.

Sin is our disregard of or resistance to God. The expression of our sin is when we do something we know deep down is wrong — like when we hurt a dear friend. The problem is that we can never be close to God now or forever because He's perfect and we're not. The religious leaders of Jesus' time put the burden on people to work really hard to offset the bad and to reach God's standards.

God made a better plan. Through Jesus, God offered us the gift of undeserved forgiveness. We call that gift "grace." How does that work? What did Jesus do for us?

Philippians 2:6-8

Though [Jesus] was God,
he did not think of equality with God
as something to cling to.
Instead, he gave up his divine privileges;
he took the humble position of a slave
and was born as a human being.
When he appeared in human form,
he humbled himself in obedience to God
and died a criminal's death on a cross.

Although He is God, Jesus decided to leave His home in heaven and come get us. Jesus lived life and suffered like us, but without ever doing anything wrong. His perfect life earned us God's "well done; good work." Jesus ended His life by voluntarily dying a criminal's death on the cross, suffering the punishment due us for our sins. But then He defeated death by coming to life once again. Right there, that moment in history, changed everything.

2 Corinthians 5:21

For God made Christ, who never sinned, to be the offering for our sin, so that we could be made right with God through Christ.

Jesus did the work for us. He lived the perfect life we can't live and died the death we should have died. He did the work so we don't have to, so we can rest in the work of His life, death, and resurrection. Jesus' work can remove the wrongs, the sin, that stands between God and each of us — not our works, but by His work on our behalf. With Jesus, we rest now and forever.

Today you can receive your rest. Today you can stop working so hard to earn people's approval because you can receive God's approval. Today you can stop struggling and share your burdens with God. Today your sins can be forgiven and never held against you. Today you can begin the most wonderful relationship ever with the God who loves you.

How About You?

Today we invite you to reflect on where you are spiritually. It can be difficult to stop and think about what is happening in our hearts and minds, so take a couple of minutes to look back over your responses during the past few weeks. Think about what has happened inside of you.

If you had to place yourself on a spectrum of where you are spiritually, where would you place yourself? What do you think about the Bible? About Jesus? As you read through the following possible places on the spectrum, you may not feel like you quite fit into any of these descriptions, but try to identify what fits most closely to where you are. This will give you a starting point to begin the conversation.

- ☐ I've liked our discussions but I'm not interested in pursuing belief in Jesus right now.

- ☐ I'm not ready to believe but I'm curious about Jesus and I want to learn more.

- ☐ I want to believe Jesus but I still have questions or fears that are holding me back.

- ☐ I'm ready to believe in and begin a relationship with Jesus and want to know how to do that.

- ☐ I believe in Jesus but feel like there are obstacles in my life that are holding me back from fully following Him.

- ☐ I follow Jesus and need some help sharing what I believe with others.

If you're willing, share with the group what your response is and why.

Next Steps

Jesus always invites us to respond to Him but if you are not ready to start a relationship with Him today that is fine. A spiritual journey is a process and we hope that the past few weeks have served you in understanding the Bible and God better... and growing closer to others.

It's awesome that you were willing to come and learn more about the Bible and Jesus. Spirituality is something that's easy to put on the back burner and it's great you've taken a risk to learn more and be challenged. You might have more questions or fears. Keep talking and praying about them with this group. Keep taking steps with others to discover who Jesus is and how He can give you rest!

Each week we've spent time at the end of our study praying. This week we want to give you an opportunity to find rest in Jesus.

Talk to God

If you are ready to accept God's gifts of grace and rest today — all you have to do is believe who Jesus is and what He did for you. Just tell God that you want His rest, His way. If you can't find the words to say, perhaps you can pray this way:

Dear God,

I understand now. I see that I've been looking anywhere but to you for rest. I see that I can't work my way to you, but that you worked your way to me. I need you and the forgiveness you give me solely through the life, death, and resurrection of Jesus Christ — who is God.

Please begin a relationship with me now. I want to turn away from self-pre-occupation and the restless effort to fix myself. Help me turn to you and to let you make me the person you want me to be, the person I was meant to be.

Amen

If you are not ready to begin following Jesus, or have been struggling with obstacles that keep you from having a relationship with Jesus, you can pray this prayer silently:

God,

Thank you that you love me. Thank you that you offer me rest. Thank you for this group and what you have taught me over the past few weeks. Help me to see the ways Jesus wants to give me His rest.

Amen

Continue the Conversation

Stonecroft has great resources and support to help you encounter Jesus and to help other women do the same. Talk to your facilitator about starting a group like this and visit www.stonecroft.org/conversations for more resources that help you have conversations about your faith story.

Still have questions? Email Stonecroft at connections@stonecroft.org.

Intro to the Bible

Let's start with this basic question: "Do you have a Bible?" If not and if you want one, you can download a free Bible app on your phone or tablet. Find an app that offers the New Living Translation. This is an easy-to-understand Bible translation directly from the original languages the Bible was written in (Hebrew, Greek, and Aramaic).

If you are unfamiliar with the Bible, opening this historic book that contains hundreds of pages can be overwhelming. What are all these unusual titles — Leviticus, Lamentations, Nahum, and Thessalonians? What is a Testament?

In this study, the Bible passages are printed in the lesson for you so there's no requirement to look up verses. What's a verse, anyway? Here are some user-friendly explanations and instructions.

The Bible is divided into two sections: the **Old Testament** (39 books) and the **New Testament** (27 books). The life of Jesus ties the two together.

What is the Old Testament?

The Old Testament contains God's Holy Scriptures given to the Jewish people hundreds of years before Jesus was born on earth. This section of the Bible begins by explaining the creation of the universe and the confirmed history of Israel.

What is the New Testament?

The New Testament tells us about the life, death, and resurrection of Jesus Christ and describes the experiences of the people who carried on His work after He left earth.

Who is Jesus Christ?

Jesus means "Savior," and Christ means "Messiah" or "Anointed One." Jesus, also called the Son of God, is God in human form, according to the Bible. Jesus lived a perfect life, died on the cross for humankind's sin, and rose from the dead — all proof that He was God.

How do I look up a Bible verse?

The Bible is organized into books, chapters, and verses. When looking up a verse, observe this format: **John 3:16**. The name of the Bible book (John) comes first. You can usually find the number of the first page of that book listed on the Bible's Table of Contents.

The first number (3) is the chapter number. Each Bible book is sectioned into longer, numbered passages called "chapters."

Each chapter is then divided into smaller sections with each section (verse) containing just a few sentences. The number following the colon (16) is the verse number.

So, **John 3:16** directs you to the book of John, chapter 3, verse 16.

What are the Books of the Bible?

Old Testament

The first five books of the Bible were written by Moses and are called the *Pentateuch*. Jewish people call them the *Torah*, which means "written law."

Genesis, Exodus, Leviticus, Numbers, Deuteronomy

Historical Books contain information about the history of Israel, its kings, and its people.

Joshua, Judges, Ruth, 1 Samuel, 2 Samuel, 1 Kings, 2 Kings, 1 Chronicles, 2 Chronicles, Ezra, Nehemiah, Esther

Poetical or *Wisdom Books* express the individual experiences, lessons, and emotions of the writers.

Job, Psalms, Proverbs, Ecclesiastes, Song of Solomon

Prophetic Books contain God-given revelation of future blessings, judgments, and promises. Prophets, the men who wrote these books, were direct spokesmen for God.

Isaiah, Jeremiah, Lamentations, Ezekiel, Daniel, Hosea, Joel, Amos, Obadiah, Jonah, Micah, Nahum, Habakkuk, Zephaniah, Haggai, Zechariah, Malachi

New Testament

Gospel means "good news." The four Gospels in the Bible tell the good news of Jesus' birth, ministry, death, and resurrection.

Matthew, Mark, Luke, John

This *Historical* book tells of the spread of Christianity after Jesus' resurrection and His return to Heaven.

Acts

An *Epistle* is a letter explaining how to live the Christian life. The epistles were written by early church leaders (some were called apostles) like Paul, Peter, James, John, and an unknown writer.

Romans, 1 Corinthians, 2 Corinthians, Galatians, Ephesians, Philippians, Colossians, 1 Thessalonians, 2 Thessalonians, 1 Timothy, 2 Timothy, Titus, Philemon, Hebrews, James, 1 Peter, 2 Peter, 1 John, 2 John, 3 John, Jude

Revelation is the final book in the New Testament. This book of prophecy gives a deeper understanding of who Jesus is and what His role will be in the future.

What is "Amen"?

The people of the Bible often ended prayers or responded to announcements and declarations about God with the word "Amen." It means "so be it" or "may it be so." So when you end your prayers with Amen, it's like asking God to answer!

Resources

Rest is one of Stonecroft's *Conversations* series.

These and additional Stonecroft resources are available to you through our online store at stonecroft.org/store.

What's Brewing? 5 chapters
This study helps you filter your thoughts and attitudes through the Bible.

Pray & Play 12 devotions
Pray & Play uses inspiring devotionals to help mothers connect with God.

Who Is Jesus? 6 chapters
This small group experience helps you discover why Jesus came to earth, what He said, and what He accomplished.

What Is God Like? 6 chapters
God wants you to know Him, and that He pursues a relationship with you.

Who Is the Holy Spirit? 6 chapters
As you consider who the Holy Spirit is, you will become increasingly aware of God's activity in your life.

A New Beginning
This powerful booklet clearly explains the Good News of Jesus' life, death, and resurrection and guides a new Christian through key topics like studying the Bible and prayer.